Carols
for SA & Men

Contents

MUSIC DEPARTMENT

OXFORD
UNIVERSITY PRESS

OXFORD
UNIVERSITY PRESS

Great Clarendon Street, Oxford OX2 6DP,
United Kingdom

Oxford University Press is a department of the University of Oxford.
It furthers the University's objective of excellence in research, scholarship,
and education by publishing worldwide. Oxford is a registered trade mark of
Oxford University Press in the UK and in certain other countries

First published 2018

ISBN 978–0–19–352418–7

Music originated on Sibelius
Printed in Great Britain on acid-free paper by
Halstan & Co. Ltd, Amersham, Bucks.

All bells in paradise

*Words and music by
JOHN RUTTER

*The title line of the text is taken from the 15th-century Corpus Christi Carol.

an - gel voi - ces sing.

an - gel voi - ces sing.

an - gel voi - ces sing.

C MEN

2. Lost in awe and won - der, Doubt-ing, I asked what this

Ped. 16' off

sign might be: Christ our Mes - si - ah re - vealed in a

(+16')

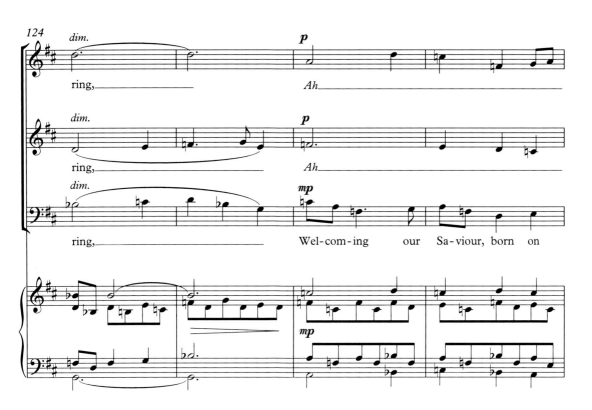

God on high' the an - gel voi - ces sing,_____ The

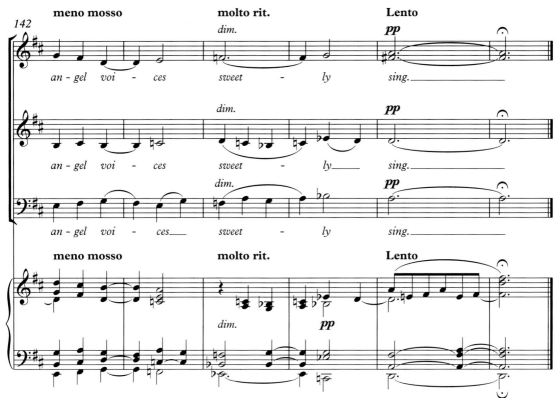

an - gel voi - ces sweet - ly sing._____

Angels' Carol

Words and music by
JOHN RUTTER

Candlelight Carol

Words and music by
JOHN RUTTER

*In verse 1, lower notes are for altos, in verse 2 for lower men's voices.

Glo-ri-a,   glo-ri-a   in ex-cel - sis De - o!

Glo - ri-a,___   glo - ri-a___   in   ex-cel-sis De - o!

dawn.   Glo - ri - a___   in ex-cel - sis De - o!

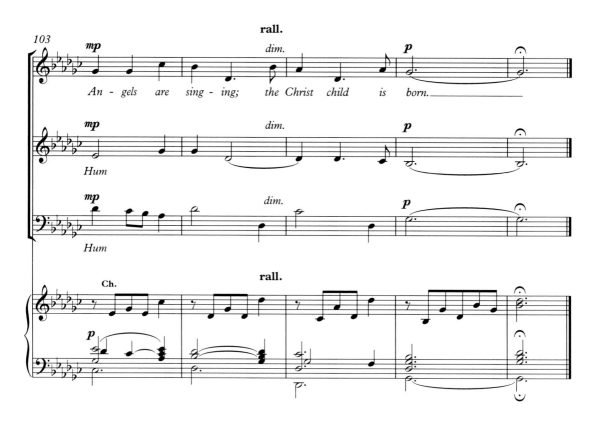

An - gels   are   sing - ing;   the Christ   child   is   born.___

Hum

Hum

Donkey Carol

Words and music by
JOHN RUTTER

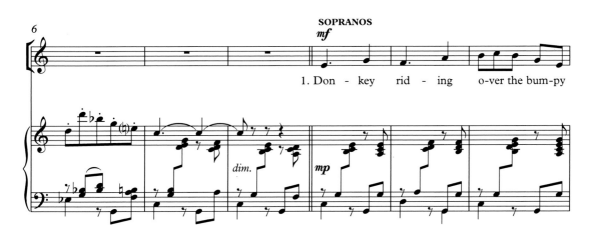

1. Don - key rid - ing o-ver the bum-py

road,___ Car - ry Ma - ry, all with her hea-vy load;___

Fol - low

una corda

-lu — ia, al — le -lu – ia, al — le -lu – ia, al — le -lu – ia, Christ is

-lu — ia, al — le -lu – ia, al — le -lu – ia, al — le -lu – ia, Christ is

-lu — ia,_____ al — le -lu – ia, al — le -lu – ia, Christ is

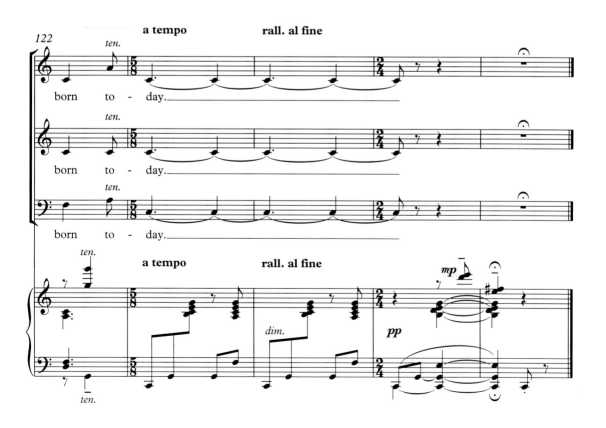

born   to - day._____

born   to - day._____

born   to - day._____

Love came down at Christmas

Words by
Christina Rossetti (1830–94)

JOHN RUTTER

Mary's Lullaby

Words and music by
JOHN RUTTER

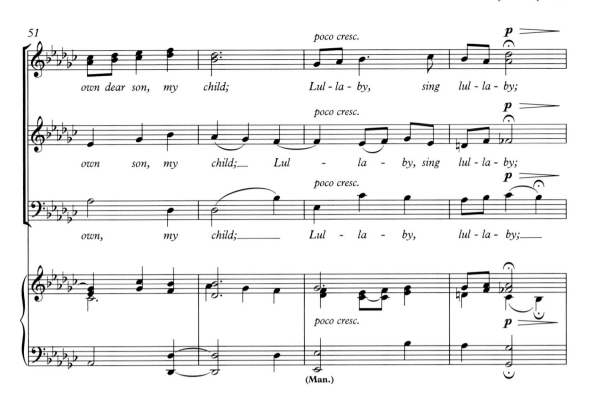

own dear son, my child; Lul - la - by, sing lul - la - by;

own son, my child;__ Lul - la - by, sing lul - la - by;

own, my child;_____ Lul - la - by, lul - la - by;__

(Man.)

Lul-la-by, my lit-tle ba - by.

Hum

Hum

(Ped.)

Star Carol

Words and music by
JOHN RUTTER

1. Sing this night, for a boy is born in Beth-le-hem,
2. An - gels bright, come from hea-ven's high-est glo - ry,

Christ our Lord in a low-ly man-ger lies;___ Bring your gifts, come and
Bear the news with its mes-sage of good cheer:___ 'Sing, re - joice, for a

*Children and/or audience may join in the melody of the refrain, which can be taught at the time of performance.

21(42) *mf lightly*

Hur-ry   to Beth - le - hem___ and see the son___ of Ma - ry.

mf lightly

mf

2nd time only

p

24 **B**

mf

p dolce

47 **C** **SOLO VOICE or SEMI-CHORUS**

p dolce e legato

3. See, he lies   in his   mo-ther's ten-der keep - ing; Je - sus Christ in her

S. A. *p dolce e legato*

Ah (or hum)

M.

p dolce e legato

C

lov-ing arms a- sleep.   Shep-herds poor, come to   wor-ship and a - dore__ him,

Of-fer their hum-ble gifts__ be-fore the son of Ma - ry.

D *p legato*
See his star   shin-ing bright   In the__ sky this__ Christ-mas Night!__ Fol-low me__

joy - ful - ly;____ Hur-ry   to Beth - le - hem____ and see the son__ of   Ma   -   ry!

4. Let us all pay our hom-age at the man- ger,

Sing   his praise on this   joy - ful Christ-mas Night;   Christ is   come, bring-ing

promise of sal - va - tion; Hur-ry to Beth - le - hem__ and see the son__ of

Ma - ry!

See his star shin- ing bright

In the sky this__ Christ-mas Night! *Fol - low me joy - ful - ly;*

Hur-ry   to Beth - le - hem___ and see the son___ of Ma   -   ry,

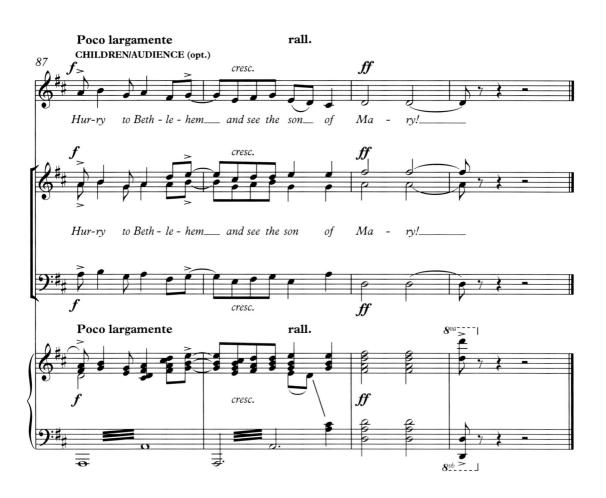

Poco largamente   **rall.**

CHILDREN/AUDIENCE (opt.)

Hur-ry   to Beth - le - hem___ and see the son___ of Ma   -   ry!___

Hur-ry   to Beth - le - hem___ and see the son   of Ma   -   ry!___

Poco largamente   **rall.**

The Very Best Time of Year

Words and music by
JOHN RUTTER

Moderato, relaxed ♩ = 84

PIANO

mp dolce

Ped. ✻ Ped. ✻ sim.

5

MEN
mp legato

Christ-mas trees and boughs of hol-ly, Yule-tide logs and mis - tle-toe;

9

SOPRANOS and ALTOS
mp

Can-dles burn-ing bright, and mea-dows frost-y white, And fa-ces in the fire - light's

rit.   **a tempo**

44

Ped.   ✳

48 **E** *mf warmly*

S.

Fa-mi-lies and friends   to - geth - er   Feel a   spe-cial kind of love   and

mf warmly

A.

Fa-mi-lies and friends   to - geth - er   Feel a   spe-cial kind of love   and

mf warmly

M.

Fa-mi-lies and friends   to - geth - er   Feel a   spe-cial kind of love   and

E

mf

51

cheer,   Shar-ing all the joys   of   Christ - mas   time –   The

cheer,   Shar-ing all the joys   of   Christ - mas   time_____ The

cheer,_____   Shar-ing all the joys   of   Christ - mas_ time –

mp

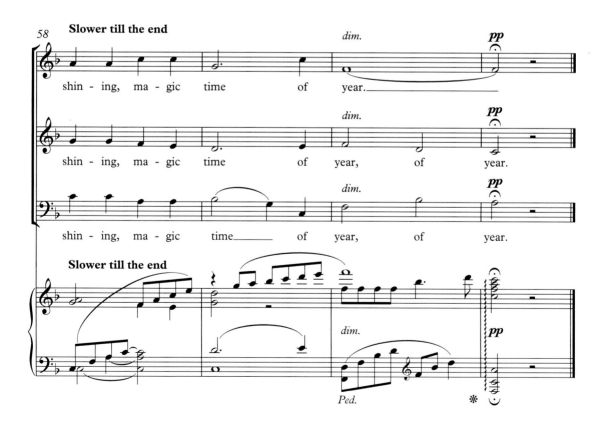

What sweeter music

*Words by
Robert Herrick
(1591–1674)

JOHN RUTTER

*Slightly abridged and altered

S.

A.
mf
Thus on the sud - den? Come and see   The cause, why

M.
mf
mea-dow new-ly shorn   Thus on the sud - den? Come and see   The cause, why

mf

mp

mp *mf*
div.
'Tis he is born,   whose quick-'ning birth   Gives life and

mp *mf*
things thus frag-rant be: 'Tis he is born, whose quick-'ning birth Gives_ life and

things thus frag-rant be:

Fl.

Man.

Index of Orchestrations

The following accompanied items are available in versions with orchestra. Full scores and instrumental parts are available on rental from the Oxford University Press Hire Library or appointed agent, and also on sale, where indicated.

All bells in paradise: 2fl, ob, 2cl, bsn, 2hn, hp, str

Angels' Carol: 2fl, ob, 2cl, bsn, 2hn, hp, str
Full score on sale (ISBN 978-0-19-351221-4)
Set of parts on sale (ISBN 978-0-19-351222-1)

Candlelight Carol: fl, ob, hp, str
Full score on sale (ISBN 978-0-19-341055-8)
Set of parts on sale (ISBN 978-0-19-341056-5)

Donkey Carol: 2fl, 2ob, 2cl, bsn, 2hn, glock, timp, hp, str
Full score on sale (ISBN 978-0-19-385781-0)
Set of parts on sale (ISBN 978-0-19-385782-7)
Also available with brass accompaniment: 4tpt, 3tbn, tba, perc

Mary's Lullaby: fl, ob, hp, str
Full score on sale (ISBN 978-0-19-385885-5)
Set of parts on sale (individual parts available separately)

Star Carol: 2fl, 2ob, 2cl, 2bsn, 2hn, 2perc, hp, str
Full score on sale (ISBN 978-0-19-385704-9)
Set of parts on sale (ISBN 978-0-19-385705-6)
Also available with brass accompaniment: 4tpt, 3tbn, tuba, timp, perc, pno or org

The Very Best Time of Year: fl, ob, hp, str
Full score on sale (ISBN 978-0-19-351257-3)
Set of parts on sale (ISBN 978-0-19-351258-0)

What sweeter music: accompaniment for strings
Full score on sale (ISBN 978-0-19-386010-0)
Set of parts on sale (individual parts available separately)